The Crafter's Design Library

Celtic

The Crafter's Design Library

Celtic

David & Charles

Dedication
For my nephew, Matthew

A DAVID & CHARLES BOOK

First published in the UK in 2003
by David & Charles

ISBN 0 7153 1441 6 (hardback)

Distributed in North America
by F&W Publications, Inc.
4700 E. Galbraith Rd.
Cincinnati, OH 45236
1-800-289-0963

ISBN 0 7153 1442 4 (paperback)

Text and artwork Copyright © Chris Down 2003
Photography Copyright © David & Charles 2003

A catalogue record for this book is available from the British Library.

commissioning editor Fiona Eaton
executive art editor Ali Myer
book designer Lisa Forrester
desk editor Jennifer Proverbs
production controller Jennifer Campbell
crafter Cheryl Owen
photographer Ginette Chapman

Printed in Singapore by KHL Printing Co Pte Ltd
for David & Charles
Brunel House, Newton Abbot, Devon

Note from the author
Many of the designs in this book are derived from ancient sources and have been adapted to make them suitable for the reader to use and create their own individual projects. Where possible, the origins of these designs have been indicated. It is often thought that all Celtic art is freely available because of its roots in the past and the presence of a large amount of source material. Unfortunately this is not the case – not all Celtic art is freely available to be used in this way. There are many new works by contemporary artists making new and innovative use of the Celtic art style; copyright law covers these new works, as any new creation would be, and should be respected as such.

David & Charles books are available from all good bookshops. In case of difficulty, write to us at David & Charles Direct, PO Box 6, Newton Abbot, TQ12 2DW quoting reference M001, or call our credit card hotline on 01626 334555.

Visit our website at www.davidandcharles.co.uk

contents

the essential techniques

the templates

Introducing Celtic art

As comeback stories go, that of Celtic art is an intriguing one. Neglected for nearly a thousand years, it dwindled to the point of obscurity. Its use had become a shadow of earlier achievements. Yet the late 20th century saw an explosion in the production and proficiency of Celtic art.

This was not an overnight reappearance. Interest in and knowledge of Celtic art had been growing for over a hundred years – a short time for a design style whose history stretches back over two and a half thousand years. Now, at the beginning of the 21st century, Celtic art is being used on a greater variety of media than ever before. As an art form, it has stood the test of time well, finding great numbers of new converts to the style. Many who appreciate Celtic art today, do so because they like what they see: at its most immediate, it looks good and is pleasing to the eye with an almost hypnotic interplay of patterns. Along with those who simply like the style of Celtic art, there are those who hold an interest in its historical basis, as a link to the past and to the people known as the Celts.

Earliest sources

The people of central Europe, whom the Greeks called Keltoi, could not have imagined the attention that would be shown to them and their way of life thousands of years later. Among the more important of their rituals were burial of the dead with objects, and making votive offerings in water to their deities. Effectively, the early Celts had been putting objects, such as swords, scabbards, axes, spear heads, helmets, rings, brooches, mirrors, flagons, drinking vessels, buckets, pottery, animals and figures out of reach, where they lay preserved, waiting to be unearthed years later. These objects, which were often covered in art, are the best evidence we have for the life of the early Celts and provide most of the examples of early Celtic art known to us today.

The first two phases of Celtic history are named after sites where objects were found. The first, Hallstatt, is from a burial site in a salt-mining settlement in Austria and dates from around the 8th century BC. The second, considered the point when the first true Celtic art appears, is referred to as La Tène after a site on Lake Neuchâtel in Switzerland where many objects were found in the waters of the lake. This period starts from around 500 BC and marks the point when the Celtic peoples started to gain the attention of their neighbours in classical Greece and Rome.

The Greeks and Romans both wrote about the Celts, but as an outsider and enemy. They only saw the 'barbarian' warrior Celt and knew little of their way of life and way of thinking. Their writings gave glimpses of the people they observed, but not the whole truth. Additionally, when the Greeks referred to the 'Keltoi', they meant all the barbarians to the north of their lands, a blanket term covering hundreds of tribes without differentiating between them.

Literacy and influences

The early Celts themselves were illiterate. They passed knowledge through a strong oral tradition leading to the reputation of the Celt as poet and storyteller. It was not until around the 6th century AD that the newly

Christianized Celts started writing, mostly the word of God, but also recording some of the orally transmitted stories. The writings give a useful insight into the mythology of the times but cannot be relied on for historical accuracy.

So, the Celts were a people who spanned from prehistory to history, their true beginnings unknown and unwritten about, only appearing from the mists of time when literate peoples noticed them. Yet, by the time of the monastic centres in Ireland, over a thousand years later, Celtic Christianity had become the seat of learning in western Europe. Pilgrims came to Ireland to learn and religious leaders left to spread the word and create new monastic centres.

Celtic art is different to classical art in that it is a non-narrative art form – there are no great tableaux of events in Celtic history laid out in carvings, yet much can still be learned. The influences on early Celtic art came from Greek, Etruscan and oriental sources. Some of this was through trade routes; for instance, wine vessels from the Mediterranean found their way north into Europe. In addition, elaborate yet unused goods were ritually placed into graves or cast into waters, indicating a people wealthy enough to create such things and a people capable of conspicuous consumption.

The Celts were also a people capable of sacking a fledgling Rome and the temple of Delphi in Greece, acts which certainly earned them notice. However, in time the Roman Empire grew in strength and domination and its control of much of Europe for hundreds of years led to the decline of the central European Celts. The Celtic centre shifted to Britain and Ireland and the people now known as the insular Celts.

Insular La Tène art continued to flourish in southern Britain until the 1st century AD, when there too Roman occupation subdued it, although it did not manage to remove it entirely. However, Ireland was not occupied by Rome, and so here the La Tène Celtic tradition continued for a few more centuries, unhindered and without outside influence.

Post-Roman history

After the Roman era, two influences radically changed the look of insular Celtic art – Christianity and the Anglo-Saxons. It is thought that ribbon interlace derives from Coptic manuscripts, the Copts being Egyptian Christians who lived in isolated desert communities. Interlaced animals came from Germanic art. The Anglo-Saxon burial

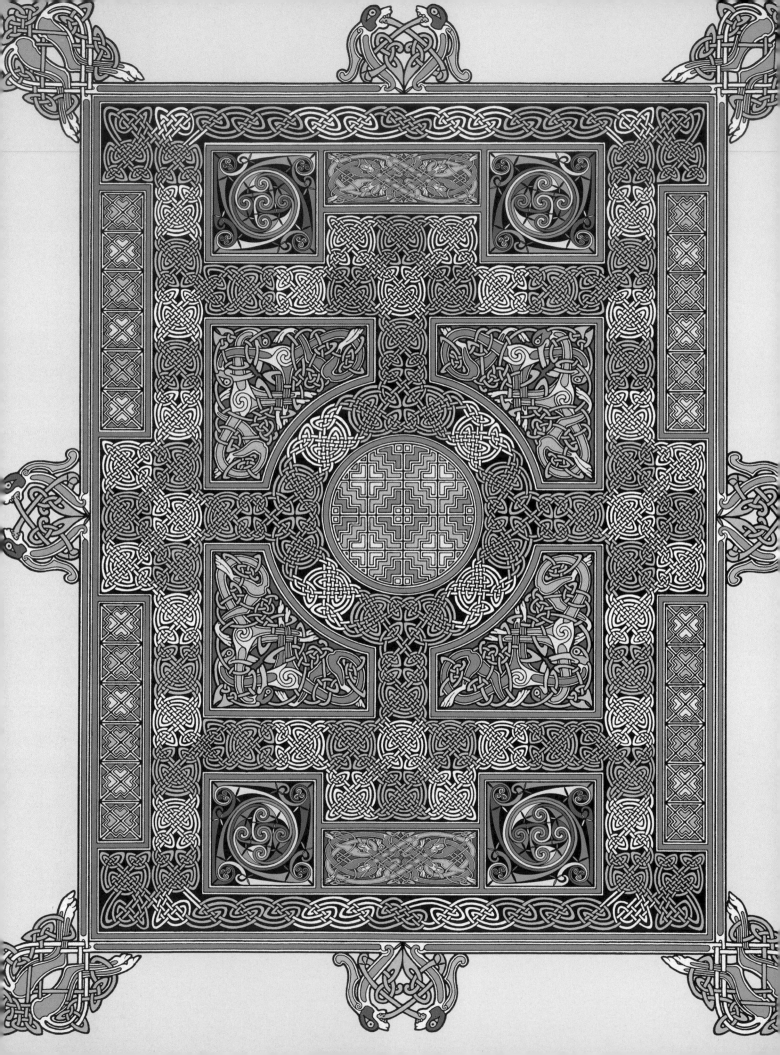

site of Sutton Hoo in eastern England contains pieces that suggest a trade in ideas, techniques and goods between the Anglo-Saxons and Celts.

These new styles found a place in the manuscript tradition of the British Isles, where they were combined with the La Tène form of Celtic design that had survived in Ireland. Some pictures also took on a narrative, as opposed to purely decorative aspect, in order to depict scenes from the Four Gospels. The most well known of the surviving illuminated manuscripts are the *Book of Kells* and the *Lindisfarne Gospels*. Both are sacred works of art that were probably used ceremonially. These two volumes alone contain an incredible wealth of Celtic motifs, patterns and designs. On their pages, there is a myriad of intricate lines and such detail that is, in places, hard to see with the naked eye. There is a wonder how such detail could be achieved without the advantages of modern technology. These books are a testament to the dedication and skill of their creators. Their work would have been the culmination of great accumulated knowledge and designs. It is still able to produce a sense of wonder and awe.

The Celts of 500 BC had taken outside influences, combined them with their own sensibilities and created an art form that was without doubt their own. The Christian insular Celts of the Irish manuscript tradition did the same a thousand years later with spectacular results. The look that is now most commonly thought of as Celtic art had arrived, an art form and style that still has broad appeal today.

Pages 6–9 show fresh, contemporary interpretations of Celtic art, using both modern and traditional colour combinations. The illustration on the facing page shows a design based on a cross-carpet page from the *Lindisfarne Gospels*.

About this book

Celtic motifs offer masses of scope to the crafter and this book is packed with a huge and diverse range of designs, from simple motifs to more complex images which will appeal to both the novice and the experienced craft worker. Many of the motifs presented here are from the two great illuminated manuscripts, the *Book of Kells* and the *Lindisfarne Gospels*. Where relevant, the historical provenance of the motifs in the templates section of the book is noted. But, few of the motifs should be considered as exact reproductions of these historical designs. They are often only part of the whole source design and have been simplified to make them more accessible.

The motifs have all been produced with the crafter in mind as clean and simple line representations of the ancient style. While some of the motifs embody the style of ancient Celtic design, others are more contemporary interpretations. Whatever your taste, chosen craft and ability, you will find something to suit you.

How to use this book

This book is aimed at those crafters, artists and others who wish to apply Celtic designs to their projects but find the creation of the designs from scratch too daunting. The book provides an extensive, themed library of Celtic motifs: from simple, swirling spirals and bold knotwork borders to striking Celtic-style lettering and fabulous beasts, figurative saints and angels, and the flowing patterns of the tree of life. The designs are ready for you to copy and transfer to your chosen craft medium.

The first part gives handy advice on how to take a motif and transfer it to a number of popular craft media, such as glass, mirrored glass, paper, card, and fabrics including cross stitch fabric. Pages 18–25 give further guidance, for the more ambitious, on using the motifs, and offers advice on simplifying and embellishing designs, combining and adapting them, using and sizing up borders, and using colour. The inspirational Project gallery (pages 26–29) of finished craft items gives yet more practical advice and plenty of ideas and inspiration on how to apply the designs to great effect.

Colour

Modern ranges of colours are immeasurably wider than those available to the original creators of Celtic art, and whether you choose to stick closely to those 'old' colours, or decide to invent your own palette, is up to you (see pages 24–25 for more advice). The Project gallery should inspire you with ideas, as well as being a showcase for some stunning and inspiring craft work based on Celtic designs.

Ideas for crafting

Glass painting The flowing lines of Celtic art lend themselves to crafts that rely on a strong outline such as glass painting, where paint is flowed within outlined shapes.

Painted crafts Figurative elements, such as Saints and Angels, work well as framed paintings. The motifs can also be painted straight onto wooden furniture, metal ware and ceramics.

Stamping Choose simple motifs for stamping, from the Knots and La Tène chapters for instance. Cut the images from fine foam, then apply to any number of surfaces, such as handmade gift cards.

Stencilling Many of the motifs can be made into stencils and applied to a huge number of craft media, or used on walls and furniture. If necessary, add 'bridges' between sections to hold the stencil together.

Découpage Celtic designs are very effective for découpage, and even the most detailed motifs can be embellished with coloured pens and pencils. Seal the finished paper design with sanding sealer on both sides, stick to your chosen surface with PVA (white) glue, then apply at least five coats of varnish.

Mosaics These can have a contemporary design, or a more ancient, traditional feel, and so are ideally suited to Celtic motifs. Tesserae are perfect for filling in large areas of a motif, while smaller pieces may be used to follow the outline of the shape.

Wire work Outline motifs with wire to make mobiles and wind chimes. This looks particularly good with the swirling lines of some of the motifs.

Candles Use appliqué wax (a thin layer of candle wax on a paper backing) available from craft shops and candlemaking suppliers. Cut a motif from the wax with a craft knife, peel off the paper and press it onto a plain candle to make an impressive decoration.

Fabric painting Use fabric paint to embellish all kinds of fabrics, including silk. A contemporary technique is to photocopy your artwork onto Lazertran paper, which can then be used to transfer the image onto materials such as T-shirts and soft furnishings.

Quilting Celtic quilting designs have always been popular. Knots and spiral motifs look particularly effective when quilted, and a Celtic border would look stunning around the edge of a bedspread.

Appliqué Many of the motifs have distinctive silhouettes, making them ideal for hand and machine appliqué.

Applying motifs to craft media

The techniques used to apply your selected Celtic motif to a particular craft media will vary depending on the surface. The following pages offer some simple advice on how to do this for the most popular craft media. Guidance is also given on how to enlarge or reduce the motif to suit your requirements.

Enlarging and reducing a motif

You may want to alter the size of your chosen motif to suit your project. See page 18 for advice on image quality before you start. There are three ways to change the size of a motif:

using a photocopier

For fast and accurate results, use a photocopier to enlarge or reduce a motif. To do this, you need to calculate your enlargement percentage. First measure the width of the image you want to end up with. Here, the motif needs to be enlarged to 90mm (3½in). Then measure the width of the original motif, which in this case is 42mm (1⅝in). Divide the first measurement by the second to find the percentage by which you need to enlarge the motif, in this instance 214%. Remember that an enlargement must always be more than 100% and a reduction less than 100%.

If you wish to photocopy an image onto tracing paper, use tracing paper that is at least 90gsm in weight. When photocopying an image from tracing paper, place the tracing paper onto the glass, and then lay a sheet of white paper on top of it. This will help to produce a clear, sharp copy.

using a grid

If you do not have access to a photocopier, it is possible to enlarge or reduce a motif by hand, using a grid. To begin, use low-tack masking tape to secure a piece of tracing paper over the original design. Draw a square or rectangle onto the tracing paper, enclosing the image (see below). Use a ruler to divide up the square or rectangle into rows of equally spaced vertical and horizontal lines. The spacing will depend upon the size and intricacy of the design. Complex designs should have lines about 1cm (⅜in) apart. Simpler ones can have lines 4cm (1½in) apart.

Now draw a square or rectangle to match your required design size, and draw a grid to correspond with the one you have just drawn over the image, as shown below. You can now begin to re-create the original image by redrawing it, square by square, at the required scale.

Transferring a motif

transferring a motif onto paper, card, wood, foam and foil

You may want to use a light box to trace an image directly onto a piece of paper or thin card. A light box is useful for tracing onto both paper and fabric, and is easy to improvize with household items. Balance a piece of clear plastic across a pile of books or furniture, and place a table lamp underneath. You are then ready to place your motif beneath paper, thin card and even some fabrics. However, this may not always be suitable for the medium you are working with, and so here is an alternative method.

First, trace the design onto tracing paper using a sharp pencil. Next, turn the tracing over and redraw on the wrong side with a soft lead pencil. Now turn the tracing over again, and use masking tape to secure it right side up onto your chosen surface. Carefully redraw the image – press firmly enough to transfer the motif, but take care not to damage the surface.

To emboss foil, simply take the original tracing and secure it to the foil surface, then rest the foil on some kitchen paper. Use an old ballpoint pen to press down on the tracing, embossing the metal below. Use the same technique on the back of the foil to produce a raised effect.

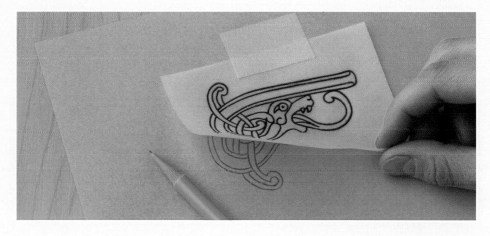

using a scanner

A third way to enlarge or reduce a motif is to scan the original image on a flatbed scanner. You can then either adjust the size using image manipulation software, or simply alter the percentage of your printout size. If the finished result is larger than the printer's capacity, some software will allow you to tile the image over several sheets of paper, which can then be joined together to form the whole image.

An image manipulation package may also allow you to alter the proportions of a motif, making it wider or narrower, for example. Take care not to distort it beyond recognition, though. Once you are happy with your image, it can be saved to be used again and again.

transferring a motif onto mirror and ceramic

Trace the motif onto tracing paper, then turn the tracing over and redraw on the wrong side using a chinagraph pencil. A chinagraph produces a waxy line that adheres well to shiny surfaces, which makes it ideal for transferring designs to coloured glass, mirrored glass and ceramic. Chinagraphs are prone to blunt quickly, but it doesn't matter if the lines are thick and heavy at this stage. Use masking tape to secure the tracing right side up onto the surface. Carefully redraw with a sharp pencil to transfer the image.

tracing a motif onto glass and acetate

Roughly cut out the motif and tape it to the underside of the acetate or glass with masking tape. It is helpful to rest glassware on a few sheets of kitchen towel for protection and to stop curved objects from rolling. The image will now show through the clear surface, and you can simply trace along the lines with glass outliner or paint directly onto the surface.

If you want to transfer an image onto opaque glass, or onto containers that are difficult to slip a motif behind, such as a bottle with a narrow neck, follow the instructions for transferring a motif onto mirror or ceramic (see page 13).

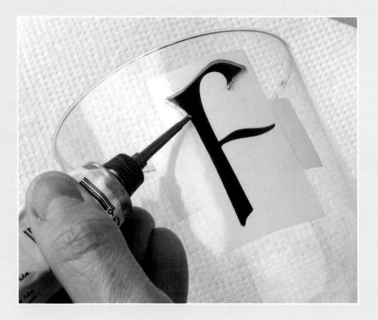

making a template for a straight sided container

If you wish to apply a continuous motif such as a border to a straight sided container, make a template of the container first. Slip a piece of tracing paper into a transparent glass container or around an opaque glass or ceramic container. Lay the paper smoothly against the surface and tape in place with masking tape. Mark the upper edge of the container with a pencil. Mark the position of the overlapping ends of the paper, or mark each side of the handle on a mug, cup or jug.

transferring a motif onto a double curvature

Motifs can be transferred onto rounded items, but will need to be adapted to fit the curves. First trace the motif, redrawing it on the underside (use a chinagraph pencil if the container is ceramic). Make cuts in the template from the edge towards the centre. Lay the motif against the surface so that the cuts slightly overlap or spread open, depending on whether the surface is convex or concave. Tape the motif in place with masking tape and transfer the design as before.

Remove the tracing and join the overlap marks, if you have made these. Measure down from the upper edge and mark the upper limit of the band on the template. Cut out the template and slip it into or around the container again to check the fit. Refer to the instructions on page 22 to adapt the band to fit the template.

making a template for a plate

1 Cut a square of tracing paper slightly larger than the diameter of the plate. Make a straight cut from one edge to the centre of the paper. Place the paper centrally on the plate or saucer and tape one cut edge across the rim. Roughly cut out a circle from the centre of the paper to help it lie flat. Smooth the paper around the rim and tape in place, overlapping the cut edges. Mark the position of the overlap.

2 Turn the plate over and draw around the circumference onto the underside of the tracing paper. Remove the paper, then measure the depth of the plate rim and mark it on the paper by measuring in from the circumference. Join the marks with a curved line.

transferring a motif onto fabric

If the fabric is lightweight and pale in colour, it may be possible to trace the motif as it is. If the fabric is heavier, or a darker colour, it may help to use a light box. Place the motif under the fabric on the surface of the light box (see page 13 to construct a home light box). As the light shines up through the motif and fabric, you should be able to see and position the motif, ready for tracing.

Alternatively, place a piece of dressmaker's carbon paper face down on the fabric, as shown below. Tape the motif on top with masking tape. Trace the design with a sharp pencil to transfer it onto the fabric. The marks made by the carbon pencil are easily wiped away.

transferring a motif onto a knitting chart

Use knitting chart paper rather than ordinary graph paper to chart a knitting design (knitted stitches are wider than they are tall and knitting chart paper is sized accordingly). Transfer the motif straight onto the knitting graph paper (see page 13 for advice on transferring onto paper). Each square on the graph paper represents a stitch. Make sure that you are happy with the number of squares in the motif, as this dictates the number of stitches in your design, and ultimately the design size. Fill in the applicable squares on the chart using appropriate coloured pens or pencils.

Use the finished chart in conjunction with a knitting pattern. Read the chart from left to right for a knit row and from right to left for a purl row. The motif can also be worked on a ready knitted item with Swiss darning. Following the chart, work the first row from right to left and the next row from left to right.

transferring a motif onto needlepoint canvas and cross stitch fabric

Designs on needlepoint canvas and cross stitch fabric can be worked either by referring to the design on a chart, or by transferring the image to the canvas or fabric and stitching over it.

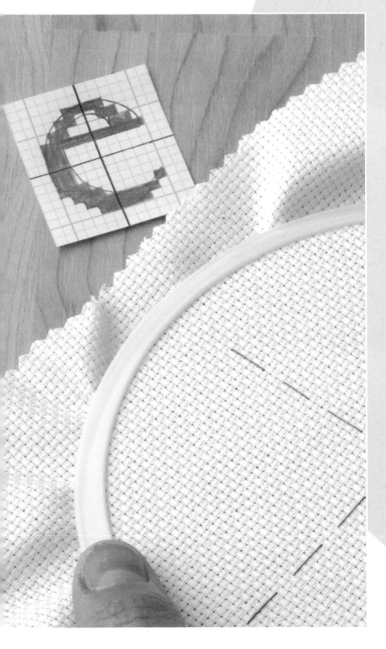

To transfer the motif onto a chart

Transfer the motif straight onto graph paper (see page 13 for advice on transferring onto paper). Each square on the graph paper represents a square of canvas mesh or Aida cross stitch fabric. Make sure that you are happy with the number of squares in the motif, as this dictates the number of stitches in your design, and ultimately the design size.

To transfer the motif directly onto canvas or fabric

An open weave canvas or light coloured fabric may allow you to trace the design onto the canvas or fabric. First, mark a small cross centrally on the motif and on the material. On a lightbox (see page 13), place the material on top of the motif, aligning the crosses. Tape in position and trace the image with a waterproof pen. Alternatively, dressmaker's carbon paper can be used to transfer a motif onto close weave canvas and cross stitch fabric (see page 16 for advice on transferring onto fabric).

Colour in the squares that the motif lines cross with coloured pencils or pens. You may want to make half-stitches where the motif outline runs through a box. Mark the centre of the design along a vertical and horizontal line (see left). Run a line of tacking stitches on the needlepoint canvas or cross stitch fabric in the same way then work the stitches referring to the chart.

Adapting and embellishing designs

The use and treatment of the motifs in this book is determined by the craft medium being used and the scale at which the motif is to be applied. As it appears in its own original form in the illuminated manuscripts, Celtic art is notable for its intricacy and fine detail. Many of the designs have been adapted from such source material and have been simplified to make them more accessible as templates. However, an understanding of the different treatments and adaptations possible can extend the application and scope of the motifs.

Line weight and thickness

Change the weight or thickness of lines to transform the look of the motifs and enable them to be used for different purposes. Sometimes, simplification of a design is called for. The size of the finished item also determines what line weight is suitable. Adjust the line weight of the motifs to suit your own needs. Below are examples of some simple changes to a basic knot motif (found on page 33).

The basic knot motif. This medium line weight is suitable for many crafts, and is ideal for enlarging or reducing the motif's size.

Increase the line weight to make the motif more suitable for crafts such as glass painting, where a strong outline is preferable.

Apply your motif to a dramatically contrasting or softer complementary background colour, depending on the desired effect.

The bold, simple nature of the motif makes it a suitable template from which to cut out a stencil for a range of craft media.

1. The basic knot pattern.

2. Add 'tram lines' to emphasize the interlace effect.

3. Interlace the 'tram lines' to create a more complex pattern.

Tram lines

One of the simplest ways to embellish a piece of knotwork is the addition of 'tram lines'. These extra lines run along the outside of the knot pattern to emphasize the interlace effect. Even the addition of a single line running through the centre of the interlace can strengthen the look of the knot pattern.

A further development from the tram line is to interlace those tram lines, turning the single ribbon of the interlace into two. Even the simplest of patterns look far more intricate if doubled up in this way – for every interlace on the original pattern there are now four.

Both the method of doubling up and basic tram lines can be used on zoomorphic bodies. However, only tram lines are suitable for spirals, as shown on page 84.

Dots

Use this simple technique to highlight and embellish your Celtic motifs. To see how effective this method is, compare the embellished motif, right, to the original on page 62. This technique is seen extensively in Celtic manuscripts as a series of red dots around the outside of an image, letters or a border. In the manuscripts this was done with red lead. Such dots are also used to form knot and zoomorphic patterns on their own, or are added between the full-colour letters and images to act as a background; one page in the *Lindisfarne Gospels* has over 10,000 such dots.

Creating new looks

Repetition and symmetry

Both repetition and symmetry play an important part in Celtic designs; the cross-carpet pages in the *Lindisfarne Gospels* are a prime example of this. Basic knot borders rely on repetition and symmetry to create their full effect. On a smaller scale, combining a motif by repeating it can create extra interest. The image right, from page 68, is essentially one dog repeated four times, making a circular shape and an internal star-like shape. Only one accurate section need ever be drawn out, which can then be repeated to form the complete design (see pages 22–23).

Mirroring a basic motif is another common feature. When this occurs, the order of the interlace on the mirrored object is reversed; that is, if a knot goes over on one side it goes under on the mirrored side, and vice versa. The bird motifs, far right facing, show simple examples of this effect.

The images towards the end of each template chapter (except the Alphabet) become more complex, and show many examples of how both repetition and symmetry add depth and interest to even the simplest motif.

left: Two designs created by repeating the same triangular motif (page 77, top). The top design uses two repeats, while the design below uses four.

Combining motifs

It is possible to combine motifs to create new designs. For instance, any circular motif can be placed in a circular border. The design below takes this idea further; the ubiquitous knot from page 50 is used to make the border, using the circular border method from page 23, joined with two knot strips to form the cross shape in the circle. Joining those various bits together where the cross pieces break into the circular border, is the most demanding part of this exercise. This particular knot pattern makes this combination easier to create than some of the more complex ones, and is one of the reasons it is often used. The repeated quadrant is from page 74.

above: A combination of the circular border created on page 23 and a motif from page 66.

Altering the shape

The shape of the design can also be altered to suit a particular purpose. At its simplest this can involve stretching or compressing a design. If this is done slightly, no great change is required. If more change is needed, simply stretching the images results in a distorted look and a proper re-draw is required in order for curves and shapes to look right.

left: A combination of motifs has been used to dramatic effect, creating a unique and intricate image.

right: The birds design has been simplified, then stretched vertically to give a different look, above right.

Using and adapting border designs

Borders and strips are in essence made from repeated basic units or blocks of pattern. To create a simple strip of knotwork, simply group together the required number of patterns with the addition of end pieces as supplied on pages 50–57. Knot borders are used in the worked examples, although the same principles apply to zoomorphic patterns. For any border, an understanding of geometry as well as use of ruler and compasses is required.

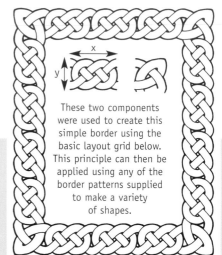

These two components were used to create this simple border using the basic layout grid below. This principle can then be applied using any of the border patterns supplied to make a variety of shapes.

Forming a rectangular border

To make a border a specific size, a degree of trial and error is needed to find the knot pattern that fits best and how many repeats of the pattern are needed. The important factor is the ratio of the length (x) and width (y) of the knot pattern as shown in the illustrations below. In this case the ratio is 1.5 – different patterns will have different ratios.

In this worked example, a border is required to decorate a frame. The internal dimensions of the border are known.

1 Divide the width of the internal border into three blocks of the knot pattern. This gives you the x measurement. Divide x by 1.5 to give y.

2 Draw the knot pattern out to that size, following the steps a–d, below. Now trace your pattern out onto each rectangle around the frame and fill in the corner pieces from the supplied motifs.

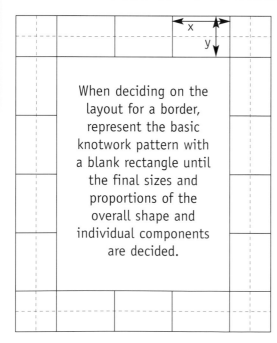

When deciding on the layout for a border, represent the basic knotwork pattern with a blank rectangle until the final sizes and proportions of the overall shape and individual components are decided.

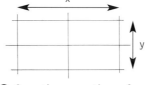

a Once the proportions of the knot segment have been determined, draw a rectangle and bisect it horizontally and vertically.

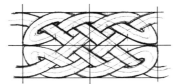

c Sketch in the order of the interlace, then adjust the lines to make the pattern as symmetrical as possible. Note the extra guidelines to help with this process.

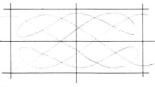

b Lightly draw out the approximate shape for the basic knot in the rectangle shape.

d Carefully trace through the completed pattern, making sure that the effect of the ribbon flowing through evenly has been created.

Stretching patterns to fit

In the example above, the frame happens to be exactly four patterns high. With a different project, the same repeated knot pattern may not fit so precisely, so stretch the knot pattern to fit by changing the ratio of x to y. Only do this by a small amount, or the pattern will look distorted. Experiment with patterns of different ratios to find the most suitable one – this process will become easier with practise.

Forming a curved border

The principles of building a rectangular border can also be applied to circles, ellipses or irregular curved shapes. These are, in fact, simpler than rectangular borders since no corner pieces are required. The two main stages for producing a circular border are similar to the instructions opposite. As with rectangular borders, the knot pattern can be represented with a blank box until the layout is confirmed, and here the circle is divided into 12 of these segments.

1 Draw the centre circle of the knotwork (the dotted line) first.

2 Divide the circle into 30° segments to give 12 repeats of the basic knot unit (giving a total of 360°). The number of repeats will determine how thick the knot band will be, more repeats giving a thinner band.

3 The distance between two intersects of the centre line gives the length of the basic unit. From this the width of the knot band can be calculated. Here, the ordinary knot pattern has a ratio of 1.5, so the length measured divided by 1.5 gives the width. From this, draw the two outer boundaries of the border, resulting in a template.

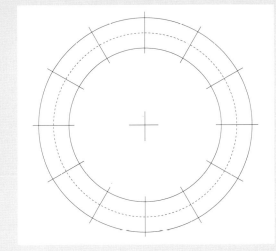

4 Use the method outlined on the facing page to draw out a single curved segment as accurately as possible; this is best done on a second piece of layout paper. When complete, place this under one segment on the main design and trace it out.

5 Repeat this process around the circle until the template is complete. The template can then be used to transfer the design onto the required media using the techniques outlined earlier in this chapter.

With both circular and rectangular borders, the vital part is getting the layout right before any knotwork is drawn; precision and accuracy are fundamental. The process of drawing a single segment then tracing it onto the layout saves having to go to first principles at every stage of the border.

Using a computer

The easiest way to create a border design is with a computer, scanner and printer. Once the layout of blank boxes has been produced, draw one knot segment accurately and scan it into the computer. Copy and paste this segment repeatedly to produce the final image. This can then be expanded, contracted and stretched to fit a particular shape quite easily and printed out for use as a template.

Using colour

The colours used originally for Celtic art were limited to the few pigments available at the time. Obtaining these was not always straightforward – the most exotic pigment used in the *Lindisfarne Gospels* was derived from blue lapis lazuli, which was only available from the foothills of the Himalayas. Not only is this an indication of the extent of trade at the time, but it also demonstrates the value placed on the manuscripts, such was the willingness to seek out a material so rare and difficult to obtain.

Today, the use of colour in Celtic art is the one point that is most subject to individual taste and is, in some respects, free of the past. Of course, where the design is determined by the craft medium being used, so are the colours. For instance, if you are doing a cross stitch design, the colours are limited by the threads available, so trying to match colours accurately may require some compromise.

To help you get started, some visual guidance is given here as to how the colours relate to each other in the illuminated manuscripts. Combined with reference to contemporary examples and your own ideas, you should have all the inspiration you need.

Zoomorphic images often had tram lines in a lighter, neutral colour. The fine interlace coming from top knots or tails also tended to be in a neutral colour, with the body holding the stronger colour.

One effect used frequently in the *Lindisfarne Gospels* was to alternate blocks of colour in knotwork. The colours used were yellow, blue and orange/red.

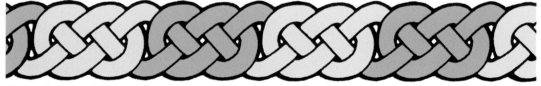

For doubled-up knotwork in the *Lindisfarne Gospels* the background was black. This highlights the intricate knotwork.

When tram lines were used, it was usual for the outer colour to be lighter and fairly neutral, such as an ochre or earth hue.

right: Where there was more than one zoomorphic body in a design, different colours were used to distinguish the bodies. This was usually done in pairs. So, even if there were a dozen bodies, there would not be a dozen different body colours, just two.

right: This segment from a design based on a *Lindisfarne Gospel* page shows the type of colours used at the time and their relation to one another.

below: Of course, there is no restriction to the sort of colours that can be used in your own designs – they are up to individual taste.

Project gallery

painted glass jug

The bold triangular spiral motif from page 85 echoes the contours of this elegant jug. Silver glass outliner was used to trace the design, which was then filled in with purple and grey shades of glass paints to match the smoky grey hue of the glass. In this case, the fine details on the motif were omitted to simplify the design, but these could be added with the silver outliner once the paint has dried.

embroidered cushion

This eminent angel, found on page 97, was worked with a variety of embroidery stitches using stranded cotton embroidery thread (floss) on silk dupion fabric. The motif was first transferred to the fabric with fabric carbon paper. The embroidery was made into a cushion, trimmed with co-ordinating bands of ribbon.

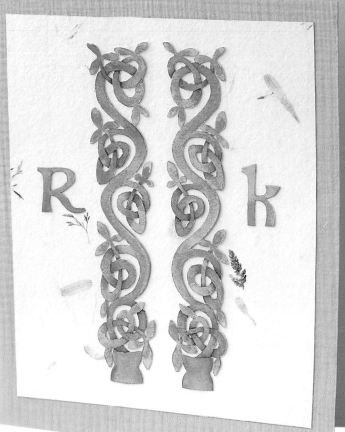

cutwork greeting card

Personalize a handcrafted greeting card by adding
the initials of the recipient. Here, letters from the
Alphabet chapter and a Tree of Life motif from page
113 were transferred to watercolour paper, along with
the tree's mirror image, with the interlacing reversed.
The drawings were cut out and painted with
watercolour paints, paying particular attention to
where the weaving effect occurred to achieve the
three-dimensional effect shown. When dry, the pieces
were glued to a piece of handmade paper featuring
delicate petals and foliage and stuck to a folded sheet
of thick textured paper.

painted silk scarf

Two motifs were combined on this smart scarf – the centre has an intertwining zoomorphic image from page 67, and the dramatic spiral border is from page 92. The motifs have been enlarged and traced with a pencil onto a white silk scarf. The scarf was stretched on a frame and the outlines traced with silk outliner (gutta). Silk paints were then applied within the outlines.

On a complex design like this, experiment with colour combinations before working on the real item.

stamped evening bag

The La Tène image from page 112 looks surprisingly contemporary when applied to this glamorous, evening bag. The pair of images were cut from fine Neoprene foam and glued to pieces of corrugated card to make stamps. Fabric paint was painted onto the stamps, which were applied to the bag before it was made up. Once the paint was dry, a dotted outline was applied with a gold relief paint pen. The bag was then made up, including padding and a smooth lining for a luxurious feel. A golden cord handle and bead edging along the lower edge added the finishing touches.

etched mirror

The understated effect on this mirror was achieved by stencilling a border using a glass etching spray. The interlaced border from page 51 was adapted to fit and traced onto tracing paper, placing 'bridges' between all the elements of the knotwork design. A transparent stencil sheet was then taped on top and the pieces cut away. The stencil was applied to the mirror with stencil mount to hold it in position. The border was sprayed with glass etching spray, left to dry and the stencil peeled off to reveal the subtle border.

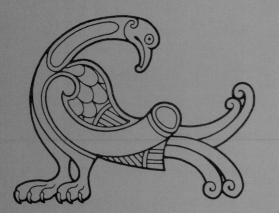

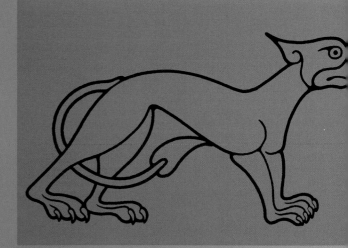

the **h**o

templates

Knots

For many, the feature most associated with Celtic art is that of interlacing knotwork. It was the last of the Celtic design elements to appear, not being seen until the 6th or 7th century AD, but it became the predominant feature of Christian-era Celtic art. In its usage, knotwork can be highly flexible, ranging from structured geometric patterns to free-form flourishes. The Celts abhorred an empty space, and knots were an ideal and adaptable space filler. The effect of knotwork is to create the impression of a woven ribbon and may be derived by an interpretation of basketwork. The more pleasing and sophisticated patterns are created from a single line.

There is only one rule that should be adhered to wherever possible – that of under followed by over. That is, if one ribbon appears to go under another, it must then go over the next one it meets and so on. That said, for some patterns it is not always possible to comply with this rule and compromises have to be made.

The triquetra, top left and right, is the most basic form of knotwork. It is most commonly seen on its own, but also forms the basis for further patterns such as bottom middle. Top right shows the triquetra doubled up, turning the single line into two (this can be done with all knotwork patterns). Bottom left and right are the same knots but with different end treatments, showing how the appearance can be altered. Top middle, middle and bottom right are from the Lindisfarne Gospels; bottom left is from the Book of Kells.

Left is a derivation from the triquetra pattern, from the Book of Kells. Middle left and right are from the Lindisfarne Gospels. Middle centre, adapted from a motif on the Chi Rho page, is from the Book of Kells, as is bottom.

*Top is from the Cannon
Tables in the Book of
Kells. Next down is from
the Lindisfarne Gospels.
The bottom three designs
are from the Book of Kells.*

Top left is from Miegle, Perthshire, Scotland. Top right is from a cross slab at St Vigeans, Perthshire, Scotland. Middle and bottom right are from the Book of Kells.

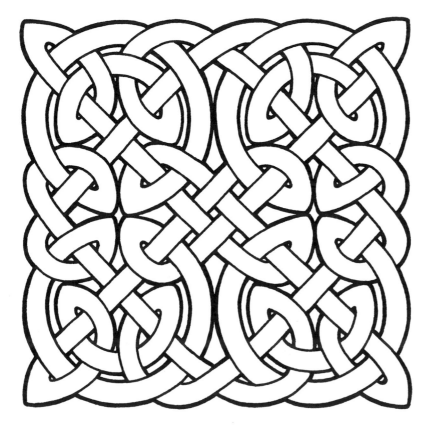

Top left is a design from a stone cross at Carndonagh, Co. Donegal, Ireland. Below right is from a portrait of St John in the Book of Kells. In the original, the knots are doubled up, but has been simplified here.

Bottom right is a design
on a cross slab from
Collieburn, Sutherland,
Scotland. Top left is the
main motif from the
Collieburn slab. This is
used as the central motif
on the cross on page 44.

The cross in Celtic art came into its own in the Christian period. The most obvious and striking crosses are those carved in stone, and these designs are inspired by such carvings.

The treatment of the crosses on these two pages can be interchanged. The central motifs on these and the next two pages have been designed from a single ribbon. This is considered the most elegant form of knotwork, but is not always possible to achieve.

This simple cross is from a cross-carpet page in the Book of Durrow. The outer knot circle has been added to make a single design.

The main knot circle here uses the same knot motif found on page 57.

These two borders were originally designed to contain pictures.

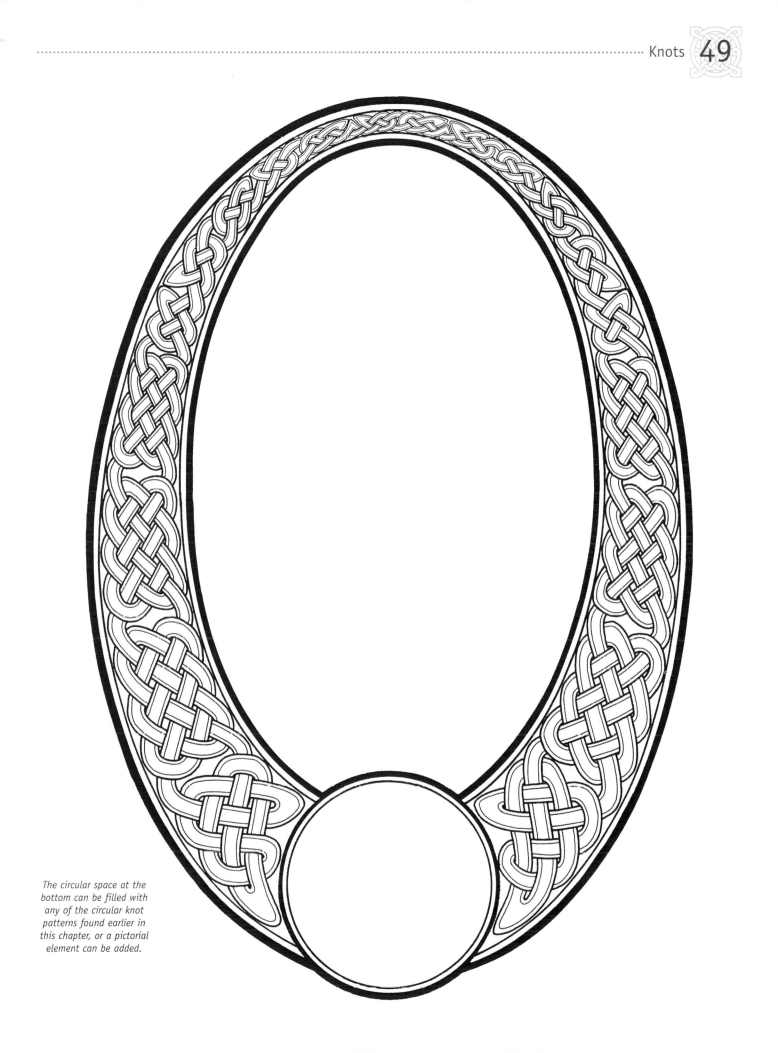

The circular space at the bottom can be filled with any of the circular knot patterns found earlier in this chapter, or a pictorial element can be added.

Knotwork is ideal for creating borders using repeated patterns. On this and the following pages are examples of basic knot patterns that can be built up to form borders or simple strips. Along with the basic units that build up the border, examples of corners and end pieces are also shown. In some cases, an extended version of the basic unit is given. This can be used to make the border fit a certain space, as you can see here in the top and bottom.

Knots do not have to be restricted to rectangular borders – circles, triangles, ellipses, crosses and combinations of all these can be created. This knot, from the Book of Kells, is particularly useful for irregular border shapes.

See pages 22–23 for the many ways in which borders can be adapted.

Pattern from the
Lindisfarne Gospels and
the Book of Kells.

The patterns here and facing are from the Book of Kells and the Lindisfarne Gospels.

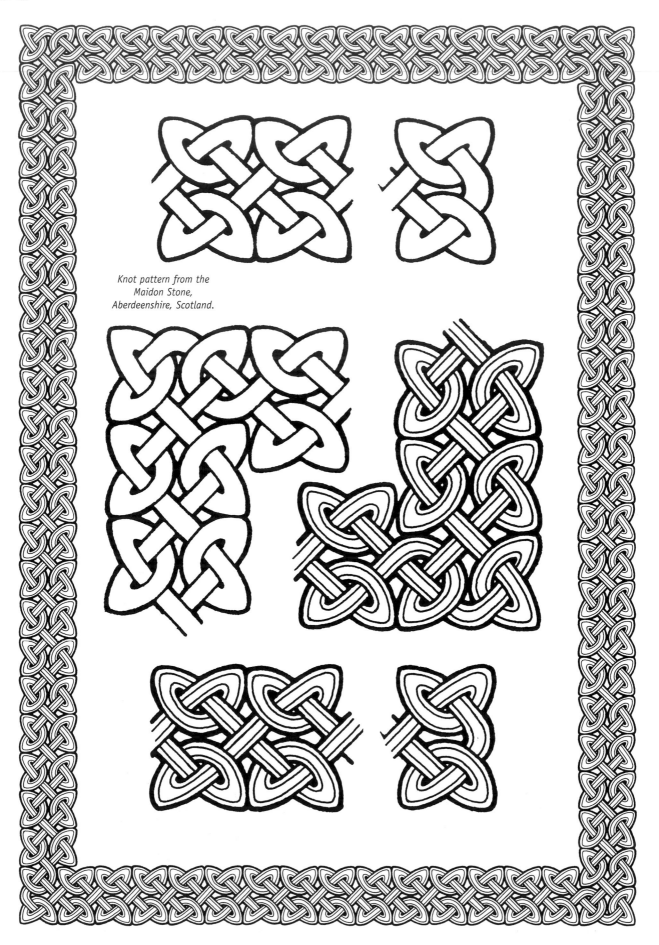

Knot pattern from the Maidon Stone, Aberdeenshire, Scotland.

A more complex version of the pattern found on the facing page. This is from the Lindisfarne Gospels.

A popular knot pattern from the Lindisfarne Gospels which appears on the major decorated pages that introduce the Gospels of St Matthew, St Mark and St John. There are three different corner treatments here, whose use can be determined by what the ratios of the sides of the rectangle are.

This pattern is from the
Lindisfarne Gospels,
introducing St Jerome's
letter to Pope Damasus,
and introducing St Mark's
Gospel. Both use the
doubled-up version of the
knot shown lower right.
Viewed as a whole, they
look highly complex, yet
mastery of the basic knot
makes the whole
achievable.

Zoomorphic

Zoomorphic designs are those that consist of animal motifs; although, strictly speaking, those with human forms are anthropomorphic, they also find their place here. Over the history of Celtic art the animals have changed: early images featured boars and horses, with associations of hunting and warfare. By the time of the manuscripts, the emphasis had shifted – beasts, birds and reptiles predominated, often incorporated into interlaced patterns.

The three animal types each have their own characteristics. The serpents are the simplest looking much like ribbon interlace but with a head and tail at either end, and their bodies retain a constant width. Adornments of fine interlace top knots can sprout from behind each eye. The birds have contorted and twisted necks sprouting from bodies that retain fairly consistent shapes with decorative feathers or patterns. Tail feathers can then extend out to fine interlace, and a single top knot can extend from the back of the head.

Given the manuscripts' biblical associations, the beasts are thought to be lions, but to all intents they look like dogs and are most often considered as such today. Their legs can join the body with a spiral, thus incorporating the three main features of later Celtic art – interlace, zoomorphic and spiral – in one image.

All these are from the Book of Kells. Top is from the arrest of Christ. Middle right is from the centre of a letter Q.

All these are from the Book of Kells. Middle is from the centre of a letter C. Bottom right is part of the letter T.

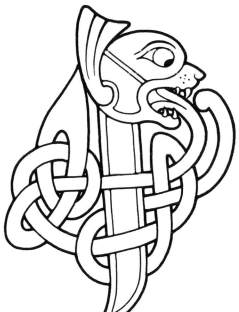

Top left is from a portrait of the Virgin and Child in the Book of Kells. Middle is from the last of the Cannon Tables in the Lindisfarne Gospels. Bottom right is from the beginning of St John's Gospel, also in the Lindisfarne Gospels. Bottom left is in a letter M from the Book of Kells.

All these are from the Book of Kells; top is the tail of a letter X.

All but top left are from the Book of Kells; top right is the tail of a letter E.

Top left, the letter D, and top right, the letter E, are both from the Book of Kells. Middle, at the beginning of St John's Gospel, and bottom, at the beginning of St Mark's Gospel, are from the Lindisfarne Gospels.

Top left is a letter E from the Book of Kells. Top right is a corner piece on a border frame from the Lindisfarne Gospels. Middle, the symbol of St John the Evangelist, and bottom left are from the Book of Kells. Bottom right is inspired by stone slabs in Scotland with carvings of horsemen.

Top right and top left are from the Book of Kells. Bottom left is derived from a motif in the Gospels of St Chad.

Top right, middle and bottom left are all from the beginning of St Matthew's Gospel in the Book of Kells. Bottom right is derived from a motif, also featured in the Book of Kells.

Above right is from the cross-carpet page introducing St Matthew's Gospel in the Lindisfarne Gospels. Below right is based on a motif from the beginning of St Mark's Gospel in the Book of Kells.

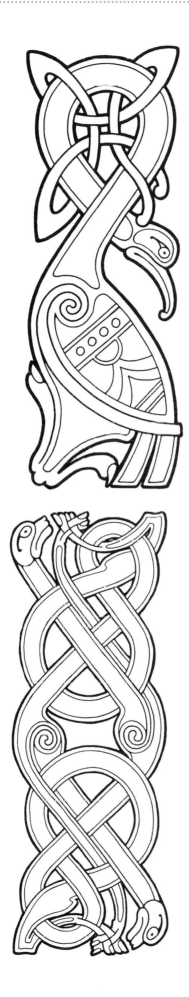

Top left is based on a motif from the cross-carpet page introducing St Luke's Gospel in the Lindisfarne Gospels. Bottom right is based on a motif from the Book of Kells. Bottom left is an elongated version of one of the designs from the previous page.

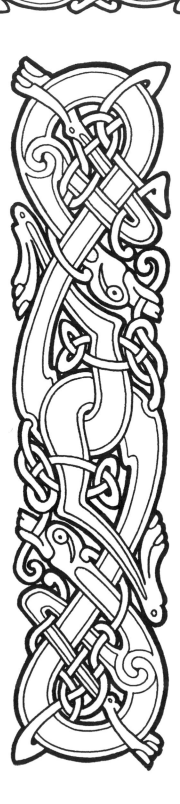

Above is a pattern from the beginning of St Matthew's Gospel in the Book of Kells. This is a more detailed version of the pattern found on page 67. Below is derived from a motif on the Virgin and Child page in the Book of Kells.

The quadrants found on these two pages can be repeated to form a circular pattern (see pages 20–21).

The man and bird motif below has an opposing interlace to that found on the facing page. This is required if the correct circular pattern is to be made.

Figure from the beginning of St Mark's Gospel in the Book of Kells.

The main bird border pattern is from St Matthew's Gospel in the Lindisfarne Gospels. The two images in the lower left are from a border in the Lindisfarne Gospels, and can also be used to create a border.

This bird border pattern is from St John's Gospel in the Lindisfarne Gospels.

The dog border is from the beginning of St Matthew's Gospel in the Lindisfarne Gospels.

Spirals

One of the earliest decorative elements known to man, the spiral is the only motif that passes from pagan early Celtic art to the later Christian period. However, the presence of the spiral declined at the end of the Christian period as interlace and zoomorphics began to dominate. The entrance stone at Newgrange in Ireland, constructed around 3200 BC, is a prime example of the spiral motif pre-dating Celtic art by thousands of years.

The spiral can be observed in nature, such as in the shell of a snail or in the curling fronds of a fern. It could have been observations such as these that imbued spirals with a symbolic meaning. The sophistication of the use of the spiral developed under the Celts beyond those used elsewhere.

The most common feature of spiral patterns in Celtic art is that groups of spirals are joined with S- or C-shaped curves. Then, as they radiate out, the spirals often expand to a trumpet or flared shape and are joined to other spirals and trumpets by an almond shape. When these factors are combined with different spiral centres and a strong sense of geometry, the result can be hypnotic.

Top left, top centre, middle left, upper middle centre and lower middle centre are all derived from the Lindisfarne Gospels.

Top left and middle are from the Book of Kells, portrait of St Matthew. Top right is from the Book of Durrow.

Top right and middle are from the Book of Kells. Bottom left is from the Aberlemno stone, Scotland. Bottom right is from the Tara Brooch, Ireland.

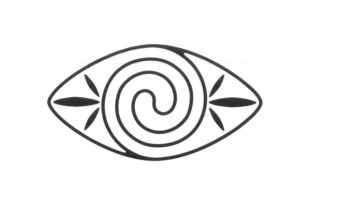

Bottom is from the
Book of Kells, portrait
of Christ.

Top is a combination of motifs from the Book of Kells and the Lindisfarne Gospels.

Top is from the Hilton of Cadboll Stone, Ross-shire, Scotland.

*Bottom is from the
Shandwick Stone,
Ross-shire, Scotland.*

Saints and Angels

With much of Celtic art the symbolism and intent behind the works is lost, but the illuminated manuscripts are an exception – the *Book of Kells* in particular has a great richness of figurative work. The evangelists, their symbols, angels, monks, the virgin Mary, Jesus and God himself all appear. Angels predominate, as they were considered an unseen but constant presence on earth.

Symbolism abounds in the *Book of Kells* – crosses, fish, lions, serpents, peacocks, chalices and vines all appear as symbols of Christ. The other key figures represented are the four evangelists, Matthew, Mark, Luke and John, with their respective symbols of man, lion, calf and eagle.

The circular disk on a pole that two of the angels are holding is called a *flabellum* and derives from the Church's eastern origin, where it was used to clear flies away during Mass. Its use in the *Book of Kells* is probably symbolic of defence against impurity.

All the images in this chapter are from the Book of Kells. Top is an angel from the second beginning of St Matthew's Gospel. Middle left is an angel from the Cannon Tables. Far right is an angel from the portrait of Christ. Bottom left is the head of Christ from the arrest of Christ.

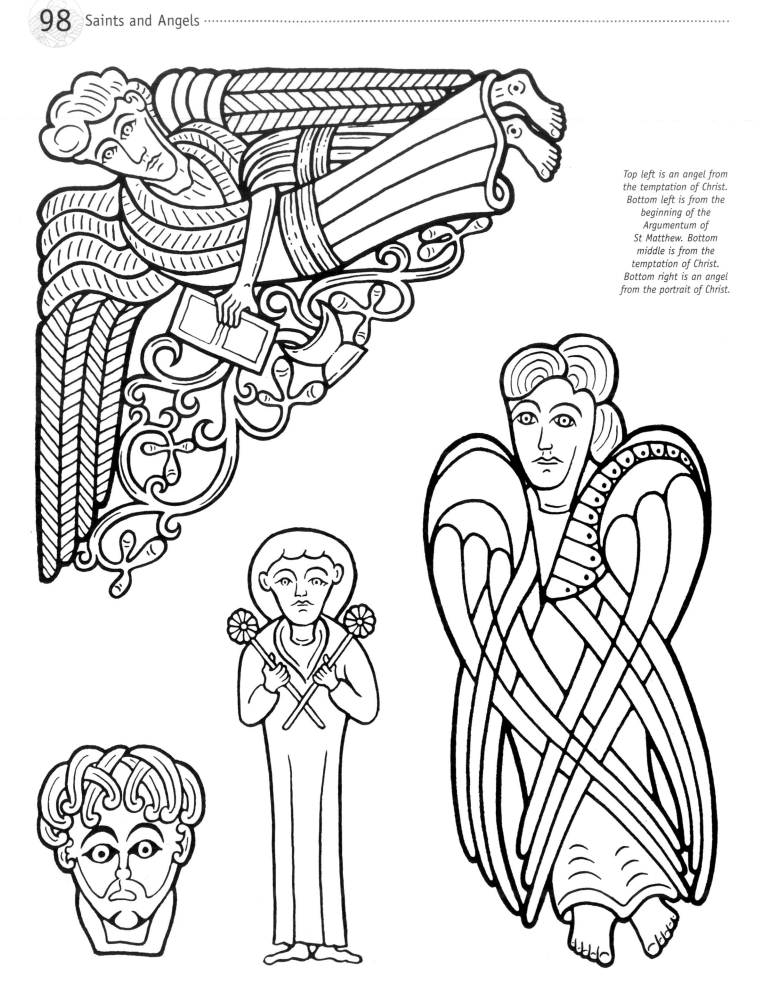

Top left is an angel from the temptation of Christ. Bottom left is from the beginning of the Argumentum of St Matthew. Bottom middle is from the temptation of Christ. Bottom right is an angel from the portrait of Christ.

The man, symbol of St Matthew.

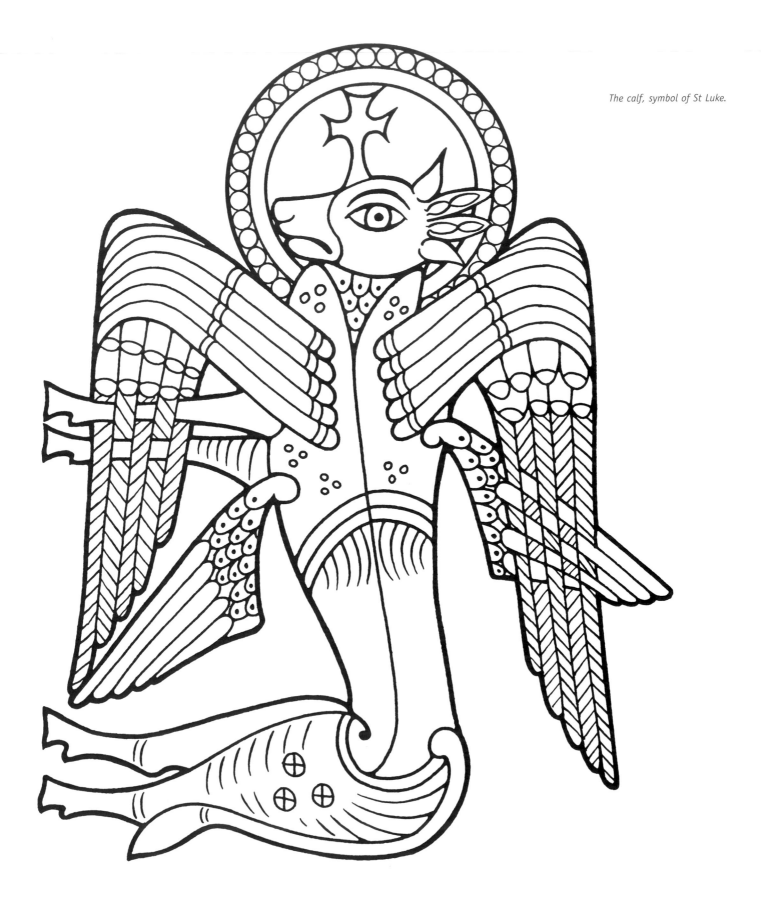

The calf, symbol of St Luke.

The eagle, symbol of
St John.

Near left is a portrait of Christ. Far left is a portrait of St Matthew.

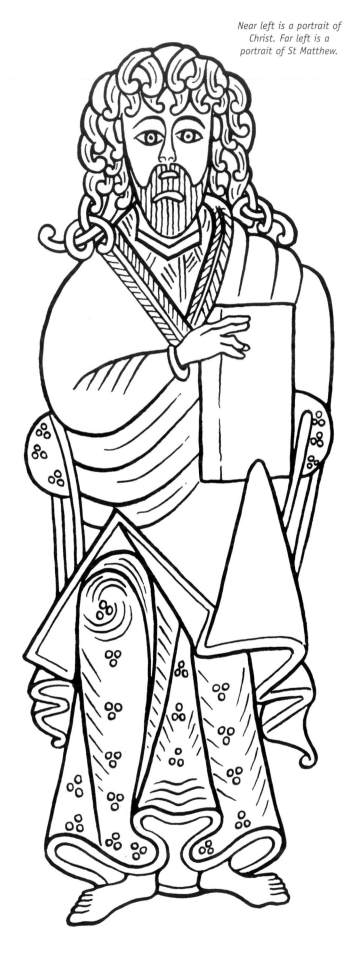

Portrait of St John.

Tree of Life

One of the rarer motifs found in later Celtic art is the Tree of Life. Its main appearance is in the *Book of Kells*, along with carved stone slabs found mostly in Scotland. In its usage in the *Book of Kells*, the Tree of Life is thought to be one of the symbols of Christ in the form of the classical vine. Grapes can often be seen among the branches.

The foliage emanates from pots or cauldrons. To the Celts, the cauldron was a powerful item. For instance, in the story of Branwen from the Welsh collection of stories the *Mabinogion*, there is a cauldron which has the property of restoring life to slain warriors. Other cauldrons in Celtic mythology have the ability to confer nourishment, status and knowledge. The Grail of Arthurian tradition is considered to have developed from the Celtic cauldron. With the combination of the vine and the cauldron, the Tree of Life is a powerful motif.

Top left, above left and near right are all from the Book of Kells. Far right is based on a fragment from a stone carving in northern England.

Far left is based on a carving on the Hilton of Cadboll cross slab, Scotland. Near left is based on a motif in the Book of Kells.

Far right is based on a design from the second beginning of St Matthew's Gospel in the Book of Kells. Near right is based on a carving on a fragment of a cross slab in northern England.

Facing middle, from the Book of Kells, is shown top and bottom on this page as a complete strip by mirroring the design. Facing bottom is also from the Book of Kells. Right is derived from a carving on Walton Cross, northern England.

La Tène

Appearing around 500 BC, La Tène art is the first true Celtic art. La Tène art adorned helmets, swords, shields, flagons, cauldrons and horse trappings, reflecting the pursuits of everyday life to the Iron Age Celt, such as hunting, fighting and drinking. In the space of a few pages it is possible only to glimpse at the wealth of material that emerged from this time, which in appearance and feel is quite different to later designs.

An interesting feature of La Tène has been termed the Cheshire Cat style, in reference to the character from *Alice's Adventures in Wonderland* that would fade in and out of view. A close look at some of the flowing patterns of the Waldalgesheim scrolls reveals shapes like eyes and noses and face-like forms.

Another type is the mirror style of southern England, three examples of which are shown on following pages. Bronze mirrors were polished on one side and decorated on the other using compass work and hatching.

La Tène art shows a simplicity yet sophistication in design that helps to disprove the nomenclature of 'barbarian', given to its creators by classical and subsequent writers.

Top left is an image stamped onto a piece of pottery from Hungary, 4th–3rd century BC. Top right is a bronze mirror back design from Aston, Hertfordshire, England, late 1st century BC – early 1st century AD. The three lower images are Waldalgesheim scrolls, named after a site in Germany, 4th century BC.

Near left is a design from an enamelled bronze harness-mount, Santon Norfolk, England, 1st century AD. Far left is derived from a design found on a sword scabbard, Lisnacrogher, Co. Antrim, Ireland.

Top left is a combination of designs on shield bosses from Polden Hills, Somerset, England, and Tal-y-Llyn Gwynedd, Wales. Top right is from a flagon handle, Waldalgesheim, Germany, 4th century BC. Bottom left is a pattern on a torque from Champagne, France, 4th–3rd century BC. Bottom right is from a bronze 'horn-cap,' from Brentford, England, 2nd–1st century BC.

Top left is derived from a bronze shield mount, Tal-y-Llyn, Gwynedd, Wales. Bottom left is a bronze mirror back, Dorton, England 1st century AD. Bottom right is derived from a pattern on a bronze helmet, Apahida, Romania, 4th–3rd century BC.

Top left is from a bronze strainer, Marne, France, 4th century BC. Top right is from a bronze plaque, Moel Hiraddug, Wales, 1st century AD. Bottom is from a horse brooch, Polden Hills, Somerset, England, 1st century AD.

*Bronze mirror back,
Holcombe, Devon,
England, 1st century AD.*

*Plaque, Weiskirchen,
Germany, late 5th –
early 4th century BC.*

Alphabet

An often overlooked part of the illuminated manuscripts is the text; in addition, they are written in Latin, making them indecipherable to most people. The *Lindisfarne Gospels* do include a translation written into the pages, but this is in Anglo-Saxon from the mid-10th century, which, though useful to the historian, does not make casual reading.

The *Book of Kells* has 680 pages, only a handful of which are the great illuminated pages. The rest is text – albeit with a wealth of decorated letters, some created from such distorted animal shapes that it can be difficult to discern the letter. The alphabet on the following pages is a combination of decorated letters from both the *Book of Kells* and the *Lindisfarne Gospels*, with modern adaptations and variations to give a complete set.

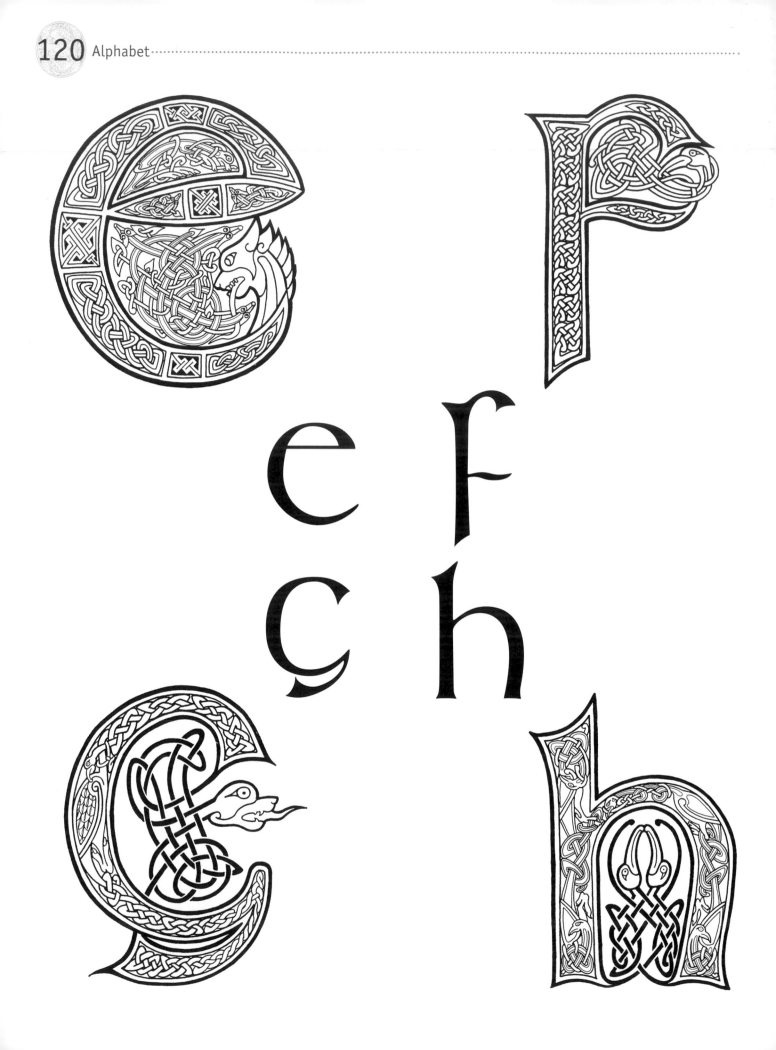

I J
K L

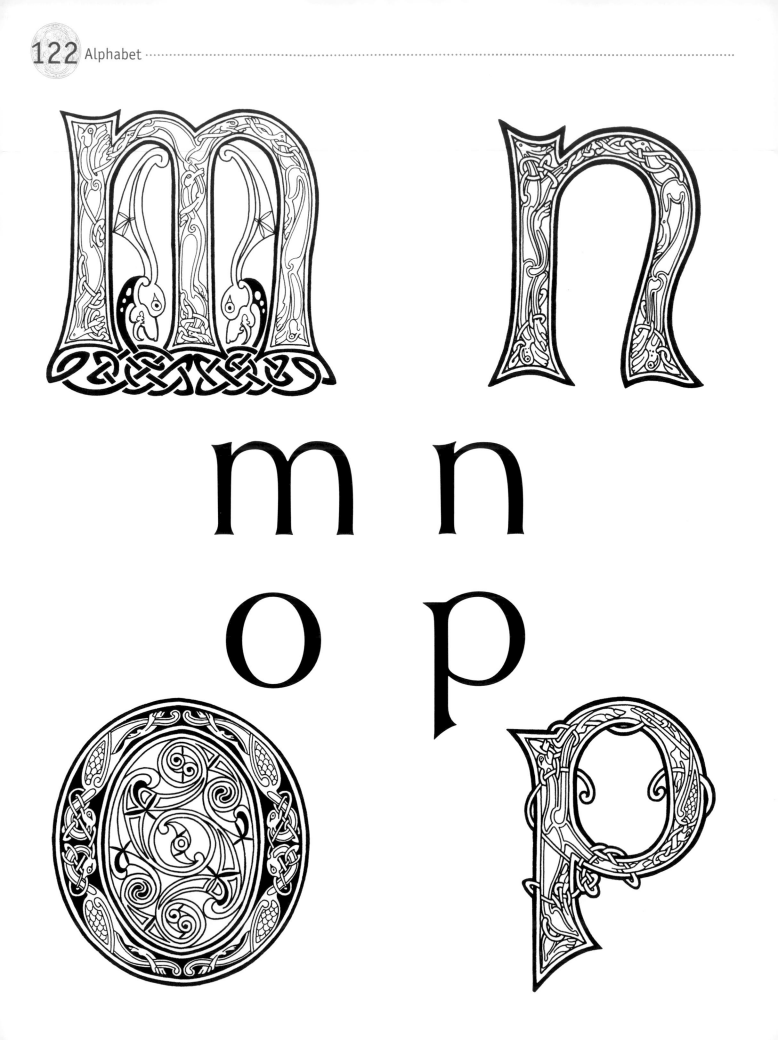

Index

About the author

Chris Down was an architectural technician for eight years before becoming a freelance illustrator, specialising in Celtic art. His first set of Celtic cards was published in 1994. Since then, he has produced further art for cards, window transparencies, mugs, coasters, jewellery boxes and wall plaques. To date he has supplied illustrations for over thirty books, although this is his first book for David & Charles. Chris lives near Salisbury, England.

Bibliography

The Book of Kells
Peter Brown, Thames and Hudson, 1980

The Book of Kells
CD-Rom, Trinity College Dublin, 2000

The Lindisfarne Gospels
Janet Backhouse, Phaidon, 1981

Celtic Art: The Methods of Construction
George Bain, Constable, 1951

Celtic Knotwork
Iain Bain, Constable, 1986

Celtic Art in Pagan and Christian Times
J. Romilly Allen, Studio Editions, 1993

Celtic Art: From Its Beginnings to the Book of Kells
Ruth and Vincent Megaw, Thames and Hudson, 1989

Early Celtic Designs
Ian Stead and Karen Hughes, British Museum Press, 1997

The Celtic World
edited Miranda J. Green, Routledge, 1995

The Celts
Nora Chadwick, Penguin Books, 1971